C. Conway Thornton

# A Ballad of Bold Burgundy

And other Verses

C. Conway Thornton

**A Ballad of Bold Burgundy**
*And other Verses*

ISBN/EAN: 9783744775465

Printed in Europe, USA, Canada, Australia, Japan

Cover: Foto ©Thomas Meinert / pixelio.de

More available books at **www.hansebooks.com**

# ·A BALLAD·

## OF

# 'BOLD BURGUNDY"

## AND OTHER VERSES

### BY

## C. CONWAY THORNTON.

ORIGINAL EDITION ENLARGED.

PRINTED FOR PRIVATE CIRCULATION.

COPENHAGEN.

PRINTED BY THIELE.

1890.

# A BALLAD

OF

# "BOLD BURGUNDY"

## AND OTHER VERSES

BY

## C. CONWAY THORNTON.

ORIGINAL EDITION ENLARGED.

PRINTED FOR PRIVATE CIRCULATION.

COPENHAGEN.

PRINTED BY THIELE.

1890

TO

HER ROYAL HIGHNESS

# THE PRINCESS OF WALES

THIS LITTLE VOLUME

IS BY GRACIOUS PERMISSION

RESPECTFULLY DEDICATED.

COPENHAGEN
MAY, 1896.

# CONTENTS.

# BOLD BURGUNDY.

## A BALLAD OF THE YEAR 1474.

### I.

Bold Burgundy is come this way:
  *(Hail, bold Burgundy!)*
He hath a mind to rob and slay;
'These peasant Swiss shall be my prey!'
  *Low lie the lances of Burgundy.*

### II.

Of Christendom thou noblest star,
  *(Hail, bold Burgundy!)*
Ripe chevalier and bolt of war,
Come, and thy fortunes we will mar!
  *Low lie the lances of Burgundy.*

### III.

Flanders, Brabant before thee fall;
  *(Hail, bold Burgundy!)*
Thy Cousin France thou mak'st thy thrall;
So is not fashion'd mankind all:
  *Low lie the lances of Burgundy.*

6

## IV.

We are the sons of Laupen fight;
*(Hail, bold Burgundy!)*
Of Sempach, of Morgarten's height:
— Amongst our hills there dwells a kite!
*Low lie the lances of Burgundy.*


## V.

Is Bubenberg unknown to thee?
*(Hail, bold Burgundy!)*
Of Pfyffer thou hast heard, may be,
His blason shows the fleur-de-lys:
*Low lie the lances of Burgundy.*


## VI.

Hallwyl and Reding, champions leal,
*(Hail, bold Burgundy!)*
Bonstetten, Erlach, Wáttenwyl;
And is not theirs right knightly steel?
*Low lie the lances of Burgundy.*


## VII.

Of such as these we've many a score,
*(Hail, bold Burgundy!)*
To join their quarrel, thousands more
Eager in soul Helvetia bore:
*Low lie the lances of Burgundy.*

## VIII.

Kaiser or King we will not know;
*(Hail, bold Burgundy!)*
Though he of Hapsburg high may show,
T'is Schweizer blood doth in him flow:
*Low lie the lances of Burgundy.*

## IX.

Then, doughty Charles, thy vaunting cease;
*(Hail, bold Burgundy!)*
With us — or Heav'n — make timely peace,
For we will shear thy Golden Fleece!
*Low lie the lances of Burgundy.*

\*
\*
\*

## X.

When Burgundy to Grandson came,
*(Hail, bold Burgundy!)*
The craven dared a deed of shame;
Then burst the Schweizer soul aflame:
*Low lie the lances of Burgundy.*

## XI.

Fell the tall keep by treachery;
*(Hail, bold Burgundy!)*
In arms our hapless folk took he,
And hanged each man upon a tree:
*Low lie the lances of Burgundy.*

## XII.

We leapt upon him, mid the vines;
  *(Hail, bold Burgundy!)*
His cannon rent our serried lines
As sweeps the whirlwind through the pines:
  *Low lie the lances of Burgundy.*


## XIII.

Rush'd, great in cheer, our yeomen staunch;
  *(Hail, bold Burgundy!)*
So brake he, as a rotten branch
Breaks neath the noontide avalanche:
  *Low lie the lances of Burgundy.*


## XIV.

Death's Angel held high feast, that day;
  *(Hail, bold Burgundy!)*
Thick on the hill-side slain men lay: —
The wine is fierce comes thence, they say!
  *Low lie the lances of Burgundy.*


## XV.

Anon, to heal his bruis'd renown,
  *(Hail, bold Burgundy!)*
His hosts beleaguered Morat town,
Till that the walls should tumble down:
  *Low lie the lances of Burgundy.*

9

## XVI.

For all his wrath, they trembled not;
*(Hail, bold Burgundy!)*
As eagles flock, so round the spot
Swift swooped each clansman patriot:
*Low lie the lances of Burgundy.*

## XVII.

Once more our warcry shook the plain;
*(Hail, bold Burgundy!)*
His engines dark dealt death in vain;
God's will was ours, the field to gain!
*Low lie the lances of Burgundy.*

## XVIII.

To th' lake, knee-deep, the grim fight drew;
*(Hail, bold Burgundy!)*
Spearpoint to spearpoint, thew to thew,
Where each man fought, he fell, or slew:
*Low lie the lances of Burgundy.*

## XIX.

The shallows wide were chok'd with dead;
*(Hail, bold Burgundy!)*
A lurid billow from them spread;
Storm sunsets show no angrier red!
*Low lie the lances of Burgundy*

## XX.

With fires of bale the night was rent;
  *(Hail, bold Burgundy!)*
To Jura's cloud-topt battlement
A huge, unearthly wail was sent.
  *Low lie the lances of Burgundy.*


## XXI.

Such haste, proud Charles, thou ow'st thy fear,
  *(Hail, bold Burgundy!)*
So small thy love for Schweizer spear,
Thou hast forgot thy household gear!
  *Low lie the lances of Burgundy.*


## XXII.

Of Flemish looms the choicest toil,
  *(Hail, bold Burgundy!)*
Silver and gold, a boundless spoil,
Ill-matcht they flout our churlish soil:
  *Low lie the lances of Burgundy.*


## XXIII.

Rude spearmen mock thy silken bed;
  *(Hail, bold Burgundy!)*
While, from hot vengeance hardly fled,
On Jura's stones thou lay'st thy head:
  *Low lie the lances of Burgundy.*

## XXIV.

Kind darkness shrouds thy woful state,
  *(Hail, bold Burgundy!)*
Where with dream-haunting wings of fate
Lone passes loud reverberate:
  *Low lie the lances of Burgundy.*

## XXV.

So for this present fare thee well;
  *(Hail, bold Burgundy!)*
Ere twice hath rung the old year's knell,
In thine own land our tale we'll tell!
  *Low lie the lances of Burgundy.*

## XXVI.

With us shall Freedom's shield repose,
  *(Hail, bold Burgundy!)*
Long as on Jungfrau's stainless snows
The dawn shall lay its crown of rose!
  *Low lie the lances of Burgundy.*

## XXVII.

Height unto height shall shout her name;
  *(Hail, bold Burgundy!)*
The streams shall bear, in silver flame,
Through all the land that proud acclaim!
  *Low lie the lances of Burgundy.*

## XXVIII.

Then mark our sooth, ye Princes all;
*(Woe, bold Burgundy!)*
Cross ye in arms our mountain wall,
As fell Duke Charles, so shall ye fall!
*Low lie the lances of Burgundy.*

# THE JUNGFRAU.

Vain in her presence is laughter or weeping,
    Naught recks her spirit of joy or of grief;
Think not to treasure thy hopes in her keeping,
    Seek not from her for thy sorrow relief:
Heart, hold thy peace then, though full to o'erflowing,
    Dry, tears, unwept, though redoubled the pain;
Here is the end of all searching and knowing,
    Here is of Silence the ultimate reign.


Queen unattainable, Whiteness entrancing,
    What leaves the Morning to woo thee undone?
Rosy the drift of his pinions advancing,
    Crowned his bright hair with the daystar alone:
Say, hath the Noonday no power to constrain thee,
    Bears thy cold brow of his kisses no trace?
Or shall the Eventide fail to enchain thee,
    Which of all love is the spirit and grace?

The orbs of the Night, in their crystalline dances,
    Thee with their chantings eternal invite;
Work they no charm for thy passionless trances,
    Bear'st thou no part in their golden delight?
Then let the thunder clouds speed them and darken,
    Fright all the vales with their fire-wingéd rain:
Thou nor to lures nor to threatenings wilt hearken,
    Changeless thou art and shalt changeless remain.


Yet thou hast loved: in the uttermost ages,
    I'the night of the Gods, before ever was man;
A love that resounds in the songs of the sages,
    The desire of the world, when Creation began:
Bowed then thy strength to its mighty foundation,
    Brake thy proud heart, beyond charming or cure,
Lonely thou sitt'st in thy vast desolation,
    Sorrowless, joyless, while time shall endure.


Hark to that voice that for mercy is calling!
    Sudden it shrills, beyond help, beyond hope:
Some rash adventurer, dizzily falling,
    Speeds to his death down the treacherous slope.
Maiden and Queen! Stay the hand of the smiter:
    Fill soft th' abyss with thy pitiful snow! —
— Perchance a thought colder, perchance a shade whiter,
    But calm in high heav'n that ineffable brow!

# THE SONG OF THE RIVER.

The river, it girdles the war-worn town
    The ramparts of rock below;
Hurtling and fast as a thunder-blast
    Its clamorous waters flow.

But soft in my chamber's haunted gloom
    It sounds through the casement wide,
In the watches white of the moonlit night,
    The cry of that sleepless tide.

So oft, so oft have I heard that song,
    Its burthen I needs must know;
Each note of the strain to my heart is plain
    As the voices of long ago: —

Pure dells of snow in a golden morn,
    Where the crystal founts abide,
Whence the sun is the first to slake his thirst,
    And the eagle alone beside: —

Then the rivulet's leap from the crag of dread
In the eyes of the laughing day,
Where half to the plain falls in silver rain,
Half hangs in a wanton spray: —

Still lakes, in the mountain's lap which lie,
As hushed in an azure dream,
But whose hearts must beat to the pulses fleet
Of the riotous madcap stream: —

Bloom laden anon, 'mid flowers and corn,
As it winds through the fragrant lea,
Aye to hasten its speed, like a spur to a steed,
Comes a far, wild thought of the sea! —

Such ever the song of the river has been
Through the round of the years gone by:
Then wherefore tonight doth a sound of affright
Those melodies underlie?

The troublous mists from the vale arise,
They have hidden the moonbeams' light,
And a vision of air, like a lady fair,
Comes floating athwart the night:

All shrouded her face and her fleeting form,
But her eyes they are bright to see;
In my bosom I feel their glance of steel
Like the spear of an enemy.

From her beck'ning hands white flow'rets fall,
  ·As strown on the face of death;
Lily blooms frail and roses pale: —
  Well the torrent may moan beneath!

For a word hath clov'n the shudd'ring night
  That hath power to rend and to burn:
A word once spoken — a heart once broken: —
  Can the ghosts of our griefs return?

And out o'er the slumbrous, ancient town,
  To the glimmering Alps away,
In a flight of despair my soul must share
  ·Nor rest till the dawning day!

# THE SHEPHERD LAD.

A MEMORY OF THE LAKE OF THUN.

Since eve, 'neath the stars serene,
Our boat on the lake had lain,
By their sleepless, luminous train
Our watches prolonged had been;
Now the daystar to rise was fain,
When there echoed a melody, falling
Sweet voiced through the floating night: —
Tis a Shepherd lad blithely calling
His flock on yon rose-hued height.

O Shepherd lad, what of the Morn?
What is't from thy crag thou seest,
Where the breath of the day blows freest,
What gleam of delight new born?
If lowly, unlearned thou beest,
So rarely thy carol is ringing,
Bright fancies thy soul must know,
Where in realms far aloft thou'rt singing
Alone, mid the silence of snow.

The stars and the fire of the cloud
  ·Thou may'st with thy runes compel,
  Thou hast learnt of the lore they tell,
Thou hast talked, neath the snowstorm's shroud,
  With the sprites, in those blasts who dwell;
And the eagle, in haunts unknown,
  Hath lent thee his glance of pride,
To leap on the peak's sheer crown
  And to stare at the sun, wide-eyed.

So high o'er our travail and weeping
  Thou walk'st, in the calm of the skies;
  Thou regard'st, with untroubléd eyes,
The depths where we faint ones are creeping,
  Nor dream'st of our longings to rise: —
It were life, to thy side to clamber,
  In the flame of the dawn to stand,
Environ'd with purple and amber,
  Supreme, o'er the glimmering land!

O green is the grass thou treadest!
  O crystal the streams that flow!
  By ways that are wild thou 'lt go
To toil, until eve be reddest,
  If mortal thy nature; but no!
Sure, of earth is thy spirit abhorrent,
  And of cloud is yon rose-hued rock
Where, to drink at a rainbow torrent,
  Thou le'adst an etherial flock!

2*

O Shepherd lad, lest we forget thee
   And our memories lose of thy strain,
   Lest we mourn for its music in vain,
In the easternmost heaven we'll set thee,
   O'er the snows of thy birthplace to reign:
Seen nighest the Dawn's white portal,
   Thy star shall our souls make strong,
While, clear mid her voices immortal,
   Shall flow thy celestial song!

# THE FUNERAL OF SIR FRANCIS ADAMS.

At Grindelwald, one morning bright,
   While the dews linger yet,
Six guides, in all their harness dight,
   ' By the inn door have met.

Careworn and seamed each honest brow,
   Their hands show many a scar,
Telling each one of a high deed done
   I'the lists of mountain war.

True princes of their gallant craft,
   Rude toil they count as air,
Of a life well lost they scorn the cost,
   The foreknown danger dare.

This one into th' abyss hath leapt
   His unskill'd charge to save:
A world below, the glacier crept,
   An the rope brake — his grave!

One hath a wounded comrade borne
　Down a huge cliff's sheer face,
Where the axe alone can bite the stone,
　The goat's hoof finds no place!

And something of the air serene
　Of those high lands they know,
The large grace of the planets' sheen,
　The white dream of the snow,

The long march of the stately clouds,
　The ice-blast's eager breath,
The silence deep of the midnight's sleep,
　The oft-heard voice of Death,

The single thought, the steadfast aim,
　The hope no strain can tire, —
Lends honour's stamp to each bent frame,
　And to each eye strange fire.

And he, who here lies still and cold,
　With them hath freely fared;
Though full his years, his faith was bold,
　And what they bade, he dared.

How oft, ere yet the kindling east
　Sang of the new-born day,
Glad as a guest to marriage feast
　He took the upward way.

How oft, at eve, in some lone hut,
  .. After long toil and stress,
He charm'd the ear with blithesome cheer
  That brook'd no weariness.


Strongly they bore him, those true arms,
  When danger frown'd confest;
How strongly now, though hot tears flow,
  They bear him to his rest!


Now mounts his soul by paths more steep
  Than all their skill hath tried;
We in the depth must pray and weep,
  .. Lord Jesu be his Guide!


His Country's flag, his life's polestar,
  Lay on his knightly bier,
And at his feet, companion meet,
  The flag o' the mountaineer;


The fire-red flag, whose crimson glow
  The staring vales know well,
When it flecks with blood the morning snow,
  Some giant's fall to tell.


Our grief, beyond the churchyard's wall,
  The torrent's ravings share;
We hear its moan as an aftertone
  Of the good pastor's prayer.

Ripe alpenrose, ye maidens' hands,
    Cast on his coffin thrice,
And with it strow the pearl of snow,
    The cloud-born edelweiss.

Not lonely sleeps he, not forlorn,
    Sure guards his peace hath found;
T''is Eiger, Schreckhorn, Wetterhorn,
    Like lions, watch around.

And when, at eve, from rose to white
    The mighty snowfields fade,
A spirit-cry from those regions high
    Sinks to that grave new-made:

One moment burns a red flush clear
    On yonder star-girt brow: —
Is it the flag o' the mountaineer
    Streams on the summit now?

# HOLGER DANSKE.

Where the fair Sound floweth
    Clasp'd 'twixt either shore,
Like a warder showeth
    Kronborg's fortress hoar.

Scarce one cable's length
    From the ramparts high,
The dark fleets in their strength
    Sail unheeding by.

Hush'd the cannon's threats,
    Once had bid them stay;
Nought but sea-smoke frets
    Walls and turrets gray.

In a vault, so deep,
    Day thereto scarce gains,
Sleeps a warrior's sleep
    Holger, Dane of Danes:

Holger, who afar
   Gainst the hosts of Spain,
In the van of war,
   Rode with Charlemagne.

All undimm'd his mail,
   All unstain'd his crest,
His hand on his brand,
   Taketh he his rest.

When each hundredth year
   Hath fulfill'd its span,
To that dungeon drear
   Flies a wild white swan.

The hero, in slumber,
   Turns his head and prays: —
'God fashion in number
   For Denmark joyous days;

'What cheer hath my Land,
   What cheer hath my Lord,
Lies Peace in his hand,
   Hath Fame sheath'd his sword?' —

'Of Bitterness and Pain
   Hath thy Land full store,
But the soul of the Dane
   Burneth as of yore!' —

Thus the swan replieth: —
By some frozen main
Then to couch him hieth
Hundred years again.

Erst in brighter strain
Was his message told,
When the fame of the Dane
Rang through deeds of gold:

Shone a gladsome beam
Through that darkling cell;
The warrior, in his dream,
Mutter'd — 'It is well'!

Twice hath th' answer spoken
Thrill'd the sleeper's breast,
Twice, the charm nigh broken
Binds his soul in rest.

First, in wrathful glee,
Hand to hilt he laid;
Now, on mailéd knee
Upright holds the blade: —

What red star shall rise,
What woes, next, for man,
When his flight through the night
Wings the wild white Swan?

# THE FOREST OF GURRE.

King Waldemar fares through the yellow beech wood,
His hounds they are stalwart, his horse it is good;
His huntsmen around him are princely and gay,
And his Queen rides, the pearl of that gallant array,
With plume in her cap and with hawk on her wrist,
Her golden locks shining like flame through the mist;
While, glad as the songs in Walhalla that ring,
Resounds with high challenge the horn of the king.


As the hammer of Thor, against giants upreared,
So wide is the sword of king Waldemar feared;
For northward and southward, o'er seas and o'er plain,
It hath gathered the folk 'neath the foot of the Dane;
Wend and Goth to him, both, as their Suzerain kneel,
And the burghers of Hansa have felt that bright steel: —
But sheath'd are its lightnings, its splendour is dim:
When Waldemar hunts, what are kingdoms to him?

Tis enough, that the forest is secret and vast,
That the quarry is lusty, and crafty, and fast,
That the merry green earth lies in glamour outroll'd,
That the air is of crystal, the sunbeams of gold;
The lake and the skies are from shadowings free,
And the eye finds no bound but the sheen of the sea:
The dawn is scarce waken'd — the night barely done —
The light fresh created — the life new begun!


Now, fierce as a torrent in mountainous flood,
Through the veins of the king flies the jubilant blood:
Thrice his bugle he windeth, and, lifting his hand,
He cries: — 'While the forest of Gurre shall stand,
Let God keep His heaven: alone let Him reign,
So this spot of fair Earth be the meed of the Dane!' --
The sweet Queen she listened: she trembled and prayed:
But the thought it was thoughten — the say it was said.


\*      \*      \*


Yet the forest of Gurre is gracious and fair,
And well may the bard take his pilgrimage there;
But let him give heed, lest the soft-fallen shades
Still find him afoot in those whispering glades;
For the breeze of the gloaming blows noisome and chill,
And the mist that ariseth forbodeth of ill;
The mighty boughs tremble, they groan in affright:
And hark! what weird horn wails despair thro the night?

Leaps a stag from the brake, which in sooth shall not tire,
For his eyes are live coals and his nostrils stream fire;
And there gallops the king in his trappings of pride,
But all bloodless his cheek — no queen by his side!
The huntsmen eke lifeless — a plague-stricken crew: —
Here's a steed for the stranger! So mount, and halloo!
Follow on! fast away! there's no halting or stay,
Lord Waldemar rides till the great Doomsday!

# THE THREE SISTERS.

## I.

There are come three Princesses all out of the North,
   *(Three are the Leopards, the Hearts are nine!)* \*)
Hand link'd in hand, they're adventuring forth:
   *(The blood of the Dane is as joyous wine!)*

## II.

Their path o'er the ocean is royally spread,
   *(Three are the Leopards, the Hearts are nine!)*
For the sun hath laid on it his locks so red;
   So they pace over at evenshine.

## III.

Full many a lover hath hasten'd to woo;
   *(Three are the Leopards, the Hearts are nine!)*
Each one flames jewell'd from bonnet to shoe,
   For each is a prince of a monarch's line.

\*) The Royal Arms of Denmark.

## IV.

Now one hath an Emperor claim'd for her right;
    *(Three are the Leopards, the Hearts are nine!)*
Her beauty is dark as the starlit night,
    The northern heavens they boast her sign.

## V.

One chooseth the Heir of the Western strand;
    *(Three are the Leopards, the Hearts are nine!)*
She is dainty and white as an ivory wand,
    And Love ever blooms where her face doth shine.

## VI.

The third loves a Prince who a crown mote wear;
    *(Three are the Leopards, the Hearts are nine!)*
Though his kingdom be spent in the troublous air,
    For gold there's her heart, and for gems, her eyne.

## VII.

Now fair o'er the lands and the silver sea,
    *(Three are the Leopards, the Hearts are nine!)*
Reigns the rose of the love of those Sisters three;
    *In heaven for aye shall their arms entwine!*

# THE HOME LAND.

Stronghold of warriors, homestead of heroes,
Mother of mighty men, Land of the North!
How glow our heartstrings when first we behold thee,
How leaps in gladness our triumph-song forth!
Joy, for thy garb of green forest deep-lying,
Joy, for thy sword-belt of foam-fretted sea,
Joy, for thy crown of red sunlight undying,
Shine, Scandinavia, lamp of the free!

Here are no aliens come to thy roof-tree,
Kinsmen in speech, as in feature and hair;
Yearns not the child for the bosom he lay in,
Knows not the mother the nursling she bare?
England! our bloodright finds here its sure token,
Let yon gray sea tell the tale of our birth;
Teuton and Gaul 'neath Rome's legions fell broken,
Spring we from Northmen, the makers of Earth!

3*

Dwellers in Asgard, awaken and answer;
  Hear, father Odin, thou foremost in place!
Thou knew'st the night which no dawn yet had quicken'd,
  Thou saw'st the daystar arise of our race:
When the last twilight the kingdoms shall darken,
  When Pow'rs of Hell to the battle shall ride,
Then to thy trumpet-call shall we not hearken,
  Worthy to fall in the van by thy side?

Still to this strand, by the magical moonlight,
  Throng shades of chieftains, their raids to renew,
Wiking and Jarl, from the banquet fresh-risen,
  Launch the long ship and set sail o'er the blue;
Burns their proud gaze with a rapt exultation,
  Seed of high empire they bear on their way,
Sown in the faith of a far generation,
  Lord o'er the lords of the forest today!

While this great world yet shall eastward be rolling,
  Oceans shall set to their glory no bar;
Strong is the march of their children undaunted,
  Urged towards the flame of eve's welcoming star:
Where the North-Speech spreads her life-giving pinions,
  There shall re-echo their jubilant voice,
There, the full strain through earth's noblest dominions,
  Peoples that triumph and hearts that rejoice!

— —

# SPRINGTIDE IN DENMARK.

The sun through many a languid land,
   Hath trail'd the gold of his burnish'd wing,
Small welcome finds he on either hand,
   ›Let me see, quoth he, what the North will bring,
   ·Where wars my rival, the Winter King,
›My soul is aweary of desert sand:‹ —
      So fares he boldly through fresh'ning skies
      To where, late-locked in her icy chain,
     A guarded jewel, the Dane-land lies
      All shrouded in mists of the Baltic main.


One shout — t'is enough! — the gloom is shaken,
   The light leaps through in a lordly stream,
Like smiling infants the isles awaken
   Whose sleep hath brought them a winsome dream;
   The ice-fields flee from the broad'ning gleam,
The loosed ships haste from the ports forsaken: —
      Far o'er blue seas their white sails bend,
      Priceless and rare the freight they boast,
     As, laden with gauds of Spring, they wend
      Unto faëry marts, on a faëry coast.

The ear is dazed with a sound of growing,
  The life-blood in all things riots amain,
Deep in lush grasses the cows are lowing
  That shiver'd but now on the naked plain;
  In one hour there waxes a season's gain,
The corn is springing, the roses blowing: —
      The trees, that were outcasts but yestere'en,
        At morn bravely ruffle in silver mail,
      At noontide have won them a kingdom green
        And have ta'en for their princelet the nigh-
                    tingale!

So short is the night, t'is a sweet surprise,
  To light's long pleasure no hindrance laying,
Like a cloud o'er the face of the day it flies
  That fleeting shade with fresh bliss repaying;
  So, when with her lover a maid is straying,
On a sudden her lashes droop, then rise: —
      The blue of the violets clust'ring under,
        The blue of the heavens serene above,
      He in her blue eyes' new-born wonder
        Reads, that down-glance it hath crown'd
                    his love!

# FOR A FAIR LADYE.

The Swallows are winging north once more,
   They cry as they come that Spring is anear;
Those merry small folk from a rose-strown shore,
   The wolds are blithe with their piping clear;
The woodlands wild ring again to their glee: —
But my heart it is fain for a fair ladye!

The grass is dappled with silver and gold,
   Daisies and daffodils prankt in their best,
A purple heaven doth the earth enfold,
   No dream of a cloud from east to west;
The bees are astir in the broad lime-tree: —
But my heart it is fain for a fair ladye!

The fishermen's fleet from the haven goes,
   Leaning white wings on the crystal air,
Their trail like a highway of silver shows
   As afar to the fortunate isles they fare;
And pouting wavelets dance o'er the sea: —
But my heart it is fain for a fair ladye!

One pillow alone for my head were soft,
That day and night might alike be blest;
Where the hill is crowned with the green church-croft,
There might I lay me and dream of rest: —
If any rest still may remain for me,
For my heart it is fain for a fair ladye!

# BY THE SEA.

The stórmwind set free o'er the emerald sea
 Stoops to roam — stoops to roam — stoops to roam;
On the deep to and fro, like to crystals of snow,
 Flies the foam — flies the foam — flies the foam.

The seabird, in pride, 'gainst the hurricane's tide
 Soars aloft — soars aloft — soars aloft;
In the frosty sunlight gleam his pinions white
 Broad and soft — broad and soft — broad and soft.

But for me still hath shone, for me pacing alone
 On the sand — on the sand — on the sand,
For the wave's fleecy crest, for the bird's snowy breast,
 A white hand — a white hand — a white hand!

# A SONG OF THE SEA.

Grudge not the Sea her dead;
　　They in fair keeping are;
Soft is each secret bed,
　　The halls are bright and rare:
Passionless, profound, eternal, through the pearly, lumi-
　　　　　　　　nous caves
With a languorous intonation flow the melancholy waves.

Grudge not the Sea her dead,
　　For she hath brought them rest;
Their earthborn cares are fled,
　　And all their dreams are blest,
For with peals of lightest laughter, softest murmurous
　　　　　　　　whispering,
Come the pitiful-eyed mermaidens, sit them down beside
　　　　　　　　and sing.

# SONNET.

A summer sunset, a plain of gold,
   A jewell'd torrent which flameth by,
   And a vision of snows in the lustrous sky,
Half Alp, half cloud, do mine eyes behold;
But, of evening's mysteries manifold,
   My heart but of one, but of one is aware,
   The delicate footfall, finer than air,
Of her that paceth the ramparts old,
Straight-limb'd, white handed, glorying there,
   Her fair, proud face lit with glows from the west,
   With a pale, sweet rose, like a star, at her breast: —
And the warm shades thrill with a strange despair,
And daylight and starlight, the Alp and the stream,
They tremble, they fade in a passionate dream!

# THE ·DRUMS.

FROM THE GERMAN OF RÜCKERT.

Hark, the drums, how merry their beat!
When to the field they call away,
Swift I harness me for the fray,
For all things else, or deep, or high,
Vain is their once imperious cry;
I cast not a backward glance thereat;
The drums so merry,
The drums so merry, so loud they beat!

Hark, the drums, how merry their beat!
After me, through the door set wide,
Father and mother in anguish cried;
Father, mother, now hush, be still,
List to you neither I can nor will;
One only sound in mine ears is great;
The drums so merry,
The drums so merry, so loud they beat!

Hark, the drums, how merry their beat;
At the street-corner, where oft of old
Loitr'ing together our loves we told,
Stands the bride-maiden and shrieks for fear
›Sorrow, ah sorrow, my bridegroom dear!‹ —
›I cannot hear thee, my sweet, my sweet!‹
The drums so merry,
The drums so merry, so loud they beat!

Hark, the drums, how merry their beat!
At my side, in the thick o' the fight,
My brother bids me his last goodnight,
And over our heads the fiery breath
Of the bullets whistles a dance of death;
My ears are proof 'gainst all their heat;
The drums so merry,
The drums so merry, so loud they beat!

Hark, the drums, how merry their beat!
What else doth call so loud in life
As the voice which biddeth us to the strife
To win high honour amongst the brave!
Though it call to death and a soldier's grave,
Never a whit heed I its threat;
The drums so merry,
The drums so merry, so loud they beat!

# ›O MOTHER SWEET.‹

FROM THE GERMAN OF RÜCKERT.

O Mother sweet,
I cannot spin,
Nor sit so quiet
This house within,
So dark and low!
The wheel, it stops,
The thread, it drops;
O Mother sweet,
Forth let me go!

The spring peeps through
The window clear;
O how can I,
Still sitting here,
Industrious be?
O let me go,
That I may know
If I can fly
Like birds so free!

O let me spy,
O let me peep,
Where breezelets sigh,
Where brooklets creep
Mid flow'rets' sheen;
Those blooms I'll take
And garlands make,
For my brown locks,
Of gayest green.

If boys come by
In wild array,
Then will I hie
And speed away,
Not stand there fast;
At the hedge side
Myself I'll hide,
Till all their riot
Be overpast!

But should some flow'rs
A good boy bring,
Which for my wreath
Were just the thing,
What then were best?
Dare I awhile,
Twixt nod and smile,
By him, sweet Mother,
Sit down and rest?

# SONG.

What I am, Sweet, an thou knewest,
  Prithee, couldst thou love me still?
Thou that sad of spirit shewest
  At the smallest thought of ill,
  Prithee, could'st thou love me still?
Or, before my deep disgrace,
Should'st thou quite avert thy face?

So some wretch, all unforgiven,
  Who by chance unheeded strays
'Mid the shining hosts of heaven,
  While his guilt his heart dismays,
  Trembling looks a hundred ways,
Till th' avenger speed at last
Him without the gate to cast.

When thy true eyes on me turn,
· From my soul all harm doth flee,
Purest hopes within me burn,
I am — what I fain would be: —
Wouldst then make a saint of me?
Look for ever on me so,
Then shall I to goodness grow!

# THE GRENADIERS AT THE WEDDING.

The Church is throng'd at the blazing noon
    With a holiday folk all kneeling,
For a maid will become a bride full soon,
    And hush'd is the organ's pealing:
When, with fife and drum, the grenadiers come
    Their way 'neath the walls a-taking,
With 'Ho! Mother Church, and hey! Mother Church,
    'What cheer at this merrymaking?'

The father, he heard, who had lost that day
    His daughter, his fondest treasure,
And his heart grew light at the clattering lay,
    Whilst his pulse beat time to its measure:
The priest one look gave his pond'rous book,
    And clean through his homily jabber'd,
And Michael, hard by in the casement high,
    Half drew his sword from the scabbard!

But the bridegroom stood, in right joyous mood,
In 'that chancel so dim and shady,
And he toss'd his head, as who should have said,
'I will dare the death for my lady!'
And the bride, whose tears, thro 'her gentle fears,
Kept flowing aye fast and faster,
Rais'd her sweet, sweet eyes with a merry surprise,
And she smiled on her lord and master!

Ah, lady dear, in each time of fear
Give a heed to that music's chiding;
With blithesome feet go thy lot to meet,
In thine own brave heart confiding:
Let the drum and fife recall through life
How on that bright day they moved you,
And the gay, gay thought their lilting brought,
When you smiled on the man who loved you!

# THE SCHOOL-INSPECTOR ABROAD.

Lines addressed to the late Mr. Matthew Arnold.

A mighty Inspector of Schools
    To Swiss land came journeying over,
Some neat educational rules
    Scarce thinking he'd chance to discover: —
School systems he'd known from his birth,
    And had view'd them in every relation;
But he'd never seen any on earth
    Like the schools of the Confederation!

At Zurich he inwardly said,
    »On a purposeless errand I reck'n I come!«
But he own'd the mistake he had made,
    When he enter'd their new Polytechnicum;
At Berne, little babies conversed,
    With composure, in French and Italian,
And he heard his own poems rehearsed
    By a six-year-old tatterdemalion!

Fatigued with his labours, at night,
 He watch'd his kind hostess the tea brew;
The dame tax'd his manners polite
 With a lecture on Sanskrit and Hebrew:
The housemaid, to beg him to pass,
 From scrubbing the staircase rose off 'a knees,
Yet couldn't refrain, saucy lass!
 . From quoting in jest Aristophanes!

The learning of great and of small
 Exceeded his utmost suspicions;
The men were philologists all,
 And the ladies were mathematicians:
The maids, at the buffets who reign,
 Could find at the very first trial *x*,
And the polish'd young guards in the train
 Ask'd for tickets in seventeen dialects!

The shock was too much for his brain,
 He has vanish'd, that mighty Inspector:
Where he's gone, not a soul can explain,
 Nor say where we ought to direct, or
How seek our respects to present,
 Excepting to put on his letters, say,
These words, 'You may him circumvent
 'In some School by the sweet Vierwaldstættersee!'

  *Berne, February, 1886.*

# A VALENTINE.

A step, that is springing, like swallows a-winging,
  An eye, that's still flinging keen glances around,
A voice, where a trill is and mirth to the fill is,
  A face, where the lilies and roses abound;
A hand, whose light swaying there's no disobeying,
  A mouth, whose soft praying the tyrant disguises: —
        Diana!
        How can a
        Dispassionate man a-
-bandon a service which boasts such sweet prizes?

Her loop'd hat so knowing, one dainty ear showing,
  So gracefully flowing her ravishing gown,
And — dream of prunella! — a boot, Cinderella
  Were unable to tell apart e'en from her own;
Her handkerchief placed so — I dote on her taste so! —
  At the belt which her waist so compactly embraces: —
        Diana!
        How can a
        Poor, ignorant man a-
-vail to describe all your fal-lals and laces?

In France she's abiding, stern winter deriding,
And England is chiding her absence in vain;
Her time she disposes in plucking of roses,
A blow to her foes is each bloom she doth gain;
For O t'is unspoken, what hearts will be broken,
(T'is mine is the token!) when home she's returning:
Diana!
How can a
Susceptible man a-
-void your bright flame, though he feel himself burning?

Of fair wildernesses, Creation possesses,
Where Nature most blesses, Provence is the queen;
But now with fresh singing the palmgroves are ringing,
A joy to light bringing that never had been:
The sunlight was glancing, the roses entrancing,
The blue waves all dancing, when there I first met
you: —
Diana!
How can a
Too fortunate man a-
-wake from such dreams, or, awaking, forget you?

*Hyères, Feb. 14, 1877.*

# A NOSEGAY.

— —

Fairylands olden mine eyes have beholden,
  Gardens all golden, adown in the West,
Where 'mid the roses the late light reposes
  Till day itself loses in rapture and rest;
Thither cares trade not, and there the sweets jade not,
There the blooms fade not, the fairest, the best!

Blossoms all shining, my fancies entwining,
  By what divining my heart do ye move?
Now in my dreaming those gardens are gleaming,
  Roam I in seeming through glades that I love;
Nor to my haunting glad laughter is wanting,
Laughter enchanting, all joyaunce above!

*Hyères, Feb. 1877.*

www.ingramcontent.com/pod-product-compliance
Lightning Source LLC
Chambersburg PA
CBHW021633270326
41931CB00008B/1009